Blessed In Battle

By

Pastor Matt Tricker

Copyright © Matthew Tricker 2018

Matthew Tricker has asserted his right under the Copyright, Designs and Patents Act 1988 to be identified as the author of this work.

All rights reserved.

No part of this publication may be reproduced or transmitted in any form or any means, electronic or mechanical, including photocopy, recording or any information storage and retrieval system, without permission in writing from the publisher.

ISBN-13:
978-1986308595

ISBN-10:
1986308596

About the Author

Pastor Matt Tricker has a vast knowledge and experience of praying for those who have been under spiritual attack. He has ministered around the world and currently pastors a Baptist Church in the South Wales valleys in the United Kingdom. Having grown up in a haunted house and reading books on witchcraft as a child he became a Christian in his teenage years. Discovering that you could not synthesize spirit contact and Christianity together he dedicated his life to following Jesus. His heart's desire is to share the gospel with those who are ensnared by the Occult and see them saved and set free by the power of Jesus Christ. When he is not ministering he enjoys the great outdoors and his family.

The Beatitudes Matthew 5:1-10

And seeing the multitudes, He went up on a mountain, and when He was seated His disciples came to Him. Then He opened His mouth and taught them, saying:

Blessed *are* the poor in spirit,
   For theirs is the kingdom of heaven.

Blessed *are* those who mourn,
   For they shall be comforted.
Blessed *are* the meek,
   For they shall inherit the earth.
Blessed *are* those who hunger and thirst for righteousness,
   For they shall be filled.
Blessed *are* the merciful,
   For they shall obtain mercy.
Blessed *are* the pure in heart,
   For they shall see God.
Blessed *are* the peacemakers,
   For they shall be called sons of God.
Blessed *are* those who are persecuted for righteousness' sake,
   For theirs is the kingdom of heaven.

Contents

Chapter 1. Blessed are the poor in spirit
page 1

Chapter 2. Blessed *are* the meek
page 11

Chapter 3. Blessed *are* those who hunger and thirst for righteousness
page 21

Chapter 4. Blessed *are* the merciful
Page 32

Chapter 5. Blessed *are* the pure in heart
Page 42

Chapter 6. Blessed *are* the peacemakers
Page 53

Chapter 7. Blessed *are* those who mourn
Page 65

Chapter 8. Blessed *are* those who are persecuted for righteousness' sake
page 75

Chapter one

Matthew 5:3

"Blessed are the poor in spirit for, For theirs is the Kingdom of heaven".

The gospel had clearly been presented, they came forward for prayer as the sun beat down on the Equator. As we prayed for individuals some shrieked and jerked as demons reluctantly left. As I stood there ministering a tall dark shadowy spirit about 12 foot tall walked behind me and those who were ministering in the heat of the day. I asked the Ugandan pastors after our outreach did they too know that a foreboding spirit had just walked behind them. They all had been aware and rejoiced that demons no matter how big or dark must flee at the name of Jesus.

When you are confronted with the demonic you know you have no physical power, intellectual skill or spiritual power of your own for self protection or to put demons to flight, as you battle an unseen world. You must know for a fact and as a living reality how great Jesus is and how great His Glory. To be used powerfully by God in deliverance ministry you must be aware of your own spiritual poverty, that you have no power of yourself, you have no physical or spiritual weapons. You cannot enter into spiritual battles unless you have come to the point of realizing that you are powerless in your own strength. If you think you can get into the boxing ring with the Devil and fight in your own strength he will knock your head off, you will lose before the bell rings. To beat the works of the enemy you must know that you have no ability or capacity in and of yourself.

When we encounter the gospel there is always a pulling down and a building up, the Holy Spirit convicts before He converts. The Holy Spirit and Gods word reveal how truly great God is. As you see the glory and greatness of God you see your own spiritual poverty, self-reliance, self-preservation, self-confidence and self assurance go out of the window. Your gifts and abilities your physical, emotional and mental strength fades into nothing as you discover an Almighty God. You learn that nothing compares to how great God is and His name is Jesus. When Simon Peter was a disciple he discovered who Jesus truly was and fell on his knees and said "Depart from me Lord for I am a sinful man" (Luke 5:8). Simon Peter knew he was a sinner and knew what it was to be empty before the Lord, as nothing in his life was greater than Jesus. Do you know how small you are compared to Almighty God? When we discover this we are in a place to receive the gift of Jesus and father God , the gift of the Holy Spirit. As our sinful pride is pulled down, our ego retreats in the presence of Jesus. When you face the demonic you need to know how great your God is. You need to be aware of how much you need Jesus personally before you go to battle. Sometimes before an exorcism I like to read about how Jesus was transfigured and revealed his glory to Peter, James and John in Matthew 17:1-13 and Luke 9:1-13 to remind me of the glory of Jesus. How Jesus' face shone like the sun and His clothes became white as light. I see from the transfiguration of Jesus how great He is and how pure He is, and I know that the devil and demons hate this. From looking at these glorious verses we see that no demon has the true splendor of Jesus and that Jesus is far greater, hallelujah. As we meditate on such verses we see how small we are and how we need Jesus. To confront that dragon we must know our nothingness compared to who the Son of God is. If we know we are poor in spirit then we are blessed because this opens up for us the Kingdom of heaven. Your spiritual poverty will lead you to complete dependence on the Lord Jesus Christ and His victory at Calvary. You will see that Jesus is greater than you and any demonic power of darkness. You cannot defeat Satan in your own strength but Jesus does as He works through you.

The greater we see our sin and poverty of spirit the more of Jesus we shall call out for and the greater the filling of the Holy Spirit. As we abandon ourselves upon Christ Jesus so we will go deeper into the Kingdom of heaven. This is wonderful news for the deliverance minister. The Kingdom of heaven is the abode of God, it is where Christ is ruling as King. Where ever the Born Again believer goes, he goes knowing he is in the kingdom of heaven, the abode of God. He knows the kingdom of heaven is where Christ is King of Kings and Lord of Lords now and in the future. The deliverance minister dwells in the abode of God and receives all the instruction he needs from the blessed Godhead.

When you walk into a haunted home where demons have been contacted, objects get thrown around the room by spirits, the rooms becomes cold and filled with a spiritual mist, family members wake up in terror with scratch marks down their backs and the pets die. You walk into that property not in your own strength but in the strength and power of Jesus Christ. You know you can do nothing but Jesus can do everything that is needed. You know how great Jesus is and His glory. You know you're in the Kingdom of heaven and you dwell in the abode of God. The relationship you have with the Savior and Deliverer of Souls puts the enemy to flight. The enemy knows he cannot harm you because of your walk with the Lord, which is complete abandonment upon Christ. You have left your own confidence behind. You are poor in spirit and now fully trust in Jesus to bring deliverance from spiritual bondage. John the Apostle wrote in 1 John 5:18 "We know that whoever is born of God does not sin; but he who has been born of God keeps himself, and the wicked one does not touch him. We know that we are of God, and the whole world lies under the sway of the wicked one".

When you are meeting with a person for an exorcism of their home or for themselves personally it's an opportunity to share how we are all poor in spirit and we all need to surrender our lives to Jesus Christ and be washed in His saving blood so we can move from darkness to light. If we kick the spirits out, the place they once occupied needs to be filled with Jesus so the demons can't come back in and make the person or home seven times worse. In the home pentagrams and dream catchers hanging up, tarot cards, Ouija boards occultist books, clothing and jewelry must be removed and if possible burnt like in the book of Acts chapter 19:11-20. Removing occult spirit inspired paraphernalia is a sign of repentance and a way of glorifying God.

Peter hurried up the narrow stairs on thread bare carpet to his dimly lit attic bedroom. The only reason he hurried was because there was no light on the attic stairs so before the bottom attic door swung shut he had to make it to his room. He slowly drifted off into a light sleep. The same events kept on happening getting more and more regular, he began to become more depressed and thoughts of suicide flittered through his mind as emotional tiredness was taking its toll. What's going on? Who is there? It's pitch dark at three in the morning. The rain beats against the window pane. The basic bedroom is cold with no heating. Peter can't move as an unseen heavy weight lies upon his chest, paralyzed with fear, straining to move but the body will not respond. His eyes move, they dart to and through the room straining into the inky cold darkness. Who is it there in the corner of the room? A dark shadowy figure that gets noticed out the corner of your eye. Peter looked again and it's gone his heart pounding in his chest, waves of cold fear sweep over him as he cannot speak but lies there as a victim of an unseen shadow of the night.

The next day a voice speaks. Peter spins around but no one is there again. The voice speaks in a friendly way. Go on jump from the attic window and you will be free like we are. On another occasion, falling into a trance and seeing wooden children playing on the lake the voice spoke again, "come and join us". The lake looked so placid and the voice was so inviting. Just as Peter was about to take a step onto the lake a passerby put his hand on Peter's shoulder and the trance was broken for now.

Sadly again that night the spirits came to Peter terrorizing him again and again. Turning the lights on and off, shaking the bed, causing their normal horrific suffocating fear. Peter would feel a large hand cover his face and press him down into the mattress. A skeptic would say,

Ah Peter you're having very bad dreams and you have a wild imagination. But Peter was fully awake and could tell very clearly the difference between reality and fantasy. He was corpus mentis and not mentally ill or addicted to illegal drugs.

One has no weapon to fight or courage to conquer such demonic entities. One is completely poor in spirit. Upon understanding his spiritual poverty Peter trusted in the Lord Jesus and began to live as one does in the abode of God, realizing he is in the King's territory, a heavenly Kingdom. Peter burnt all his occult and witchcraft books as he knew the Lord would not approve. Fully trusting in Jesus he went to bed. Again he was woken in the night by shadowy spirits, again he was paralyzed by fear and afraid, struggling to breathe, and could not speak. Peter thought the name of Jesus in his mind. As he did so he felt strength rising inside of him. The thought of the name of Jesus turned into a whisper and then he could speak the name of Jesus, in a normal tone all the time he was getting stronger. Eventually he jumped out of bed took a step towards the loathing tormenting demon and said In the NAME OF JESUS LEAVE ME ALONE AND LEAVE. The demon power immediately left and the room filled with the presence of the King. Blessed are the poor in spirit for theirs is the Kingdom of heaven. Hallelujah.

Chapter 2

Matthew 5:4

"Blessed are those who mourn for they shall be comforted".

"A Sacramento Elementary School in Portland has given permission for Satanists to host an after school club to teach about Satanism to Children as an alternative to a Christian club" announced the news reporter on Fox News.
When we encounter the Lord Jesus and a work of the Holy Spirit there is a mourning, a grieving that goes on over the sin we have committed. We wish we had never committed such sins as we see ourselves as sinners in need of a saviour. As we mourn our sin we discover that it leads us to a greater joy and freedom as we know we are forgiven by Christ and washed in His blood. The mourning and grief over sin is part of the repentance process that we go through. This is a blessing as it leads to comfort. The believer is comforted by knowing God's amazing grace, hope and glory that is yet to come in all its fullness and yet only tasted here and now. Spiritual grief opens a door for God's supernatural comfort to flow into the

deepest parts of our soul. We can find ourselves with a mixture of grief over sin and rejoicing at the same time because of the comfort that Christ gives us. We have sorrow over sin but not in an ill-tempered sullen miserable way that prevents Christ from being seen.

When the Spiritual warfare servant of Christ reads in the paper or sees on the news that Children are being recruited to learn about Satan worship it grieves his heart. When we learn that teenagers are targeted by satanic groups to join them it grieves us, especially when they instruct teenagers who have been brought up in the Christian faith at home to join them. They then delight in teaching their new converts how not to get caught by the Christian parents. They also teach the Bible is a lie and Satan never lies or murders but Jesus does. In our heart we can sigh sorrowfully as our hearts cry out to a Holy Loving God saying," Lord this is wrong, stop this, have mercy Lord". In prayer we can be on our knees as the Holy Spirit grips us with Godly sorrow as we see the work of sin in humanity and the devil pulling the strings like a puppeteer.

When the sins of those around stir your heart to mourn, you naturally begin to pray. The Greek word for mourn here in verse 4 is the strongest word possible for mourning in the Greek language, as the Greek word mourn here refers to mourning for the dead. I like the prophet Daniel as he sees the desperately sorrowful state of the people of God. Daniel was a man of faith and prayer living in the occult capital Babylon. God's people were taken to Babylon as they had sinned and fallen into idol worship. What was Daniels response? He prayed

Daniel 9:19-21

[19] O Lord, hear; O Lord, forgive; O Lord, hearken and do; defer not, for thine own sake, O my God, because thy city and thy people are called by thy name.

[20] And while I was speaking, and praying, and confessing my sin and the sin of my people Israel, and presenting my supplication before Jehovah my God for the holy mountain of my God;

[21] yea, while I was speaking in prayer, the man Gabriel, whom I had seen in the vision at the beginning, being caused to fly swiftly, touched me about the time of the evening offering.

Daniel confessed his sin and the sin of the people and then God's messenger Gabriel turned up. Daniel was not personally attacking Babylonian demons here with all prayer guns blazing, he was pulling demonic access points out from underneath them. When you ask the Lord to forgive sin you have taken away the very object demons love to use to come into people's lives. A person may have a sculpture of a demon or false god in their living room, they may not be worshipping it by burning candles and incense with an offering plate of fruit, but it can act as a spiritual anchor point for the demon to enter into that home to cause disunity amongst the family. Demons like to isolate family members to cause them more fear and terror. What is the answer? Get rid of the sinful sculpted idol and the demon has no right in your life. It's the same with pornography which can act as a visual idol. If you keep looking at porn then you open the door to an unclean spirit coming into your life, get rid of the pornography, find some accountability let the sorrow go deep into your heart and know the comfort of the Lord and his greatness. Pornography can open the door to unclean demons of lust, rape, perversion, abuse and the list goes on. We live in a sex mad society.

The fantasy idol of the mind is a most secretive seducer as no one else knows that it is there and what your mind is focused on. A spiritual psychic projection can sometimes happen through the visualization for selfish sexual self gratification causing a demonic anointing to come upon you. This can lead to rape or abuse. Hence sometimes when in the presence of another person you sometimes discern a slimy ingratiating creepiness about them, and find that some strange power fills your mind with the most impure and even unnatural sexual acts, which leave you feeling polluted and contaminated. This is because the person has opened themselves up to sexual seductive spirits which seek to corrupt and abuse you. You can be a committed Christian and your heart right with the Lord. It is nothing that you have done wrong but the nature of this perverted spirit is trying to corrupt you. Hence you do not condemn yourself for feeling unclean. But ask for the blood of Jesus to wash over you. And declare the Holiness of God in your life. You may need to get alone and pray and have a private praise time to shift the effects of this perverted sexual demon.

I have had people come into my church office

with such spirits and have felt completely spiritually violated as an immense spiritual battle takes place in the spirit realm. In the natural it just looks like me having a coffee and a chat. As soon as the person has left its time to be with the Lord Jesus who is holy and pure and has power to wash the pollution from our mind/soul.

Often in grief and mourning there is the feeling of anger. It's ok to be angry at such vile demonic perverted work as it pervades through and controls individuals and contaminates those around them. Mourning over evil in righteous anger can lead to powerful action and praying. A righteous anger at the right time is good and under the control of the Holy Spirit. If its carnal selfish anger we can be manipulated by the very demon we seek to conquer.

The spiritual warrior knows that His God is Holy hence he grieves over his or her sin and other's sins. They do not boast of a sinful past which would be prideful and the nature of Satan. They refer to the past only when needed to highlight the grace and depth of God's love and forgiveness from which they have found comfort.

When we sit down with survivors of Satanic

ritual abuse we must be prepared to weep and mourn over the sinful diabolical acts that were committed against them. When such trauma and abuse were committed God was grieved and God felt their pain.

The phone rang with a message to visit a house next to the train lines to pray where many had taken their lives by jumping from the bridge. A young man fresh out of prison had contacted us and said the house was full of spirits which tried to communicate with his thoughts. Sandra and I arrived at his home. It was pouring down with rain as the wind whipped up the heavy raindrops that hit you in the face like machine-gun fire. The shopping centre was dark and deserted. We knew that some practicing witches lived a few houses away in the street. As we stepped into the house it was like the force of a magnet trying to push you away. We listened to the man's stories of how he had found Jesus in prison. We began to pray. As we did Sandra began to weep silently and she explained how she had lived in that very house. She had used the house for witchcraft and spirit work plus opening up psychic doorways into the spirit realm for spirits to come through. She wept about the adulterous relationships she had had in that place. Sandra had been set free from her past and forgiven by the Lord Jesus. Returning to her old home stirred a sense of grief over her past sin and a deep sense of gratitude to the Lord Jesus for his deep work and comforted to know of Christ's grace and love towards her.

The spirits were expelled in the name of Jesus. The young man eventually moved away and is attending a Baptist Church. The witches in the street received Christian literature a few months later, Sandra goes deeper with the Lord knowing that He is a God who comforts the ones who rescues us out of terrible filth and bondage. Blessed are they in battle.

Chapter 3

Matthew 5:5

"Blessed are the meek, For they shall inherit the earth".

He came out the health food shop with a bag of sunflower seeds. His thinning curly hair sparkling in the Sun. The dancing wind bringing refreshment in the sticky heat of the day. His eyes were totally at peace with himself and the universe like deep pools of infinity leading to another calmer, better world. He did not seem to walk down the street but looked as if he was floating in perfect serenity. As you drew near to this man with a connection to the earth so deep, you discovered the intoxication of his meek passive energy leaving you in a day dream as if nothing seemed to really matter. He ran the local meditation group which his whole being seemed to say come and join us for we are all one together.
Within the Spiritual and New Age groups we often find a false meekness that seeks to draw you into its deadly snare like falling asleep to a lullaby. Every person can seem so laid back

with a passive connectedness achieved through meditation. You would believe these are the most gentle people in the world striving for global peace and world unity. However start talking about how Jesus is the only way to heaven and the Bible is God's truth and more than a few feathers can get ruffled and voices get raised.

Biblical meekness is like a humble gentleness that is strong and under control due to knowing Christ's greatness and understanding ourselves as poor in spirit. David in the Bible could have taken King Saul's life twice (1 Samuel 24:10, 26:8-10) but David did not do so, hence David shows great strength under control because he knows his God is greater and is in control of every circumstance. This meekness prevents us from looking down on those into the occult in a derogative manner but to view them as ourselves, lost sinners going our own way needing a work of Jesus in their hearts. Out of meekness we have a correct loving attitude that is humble and respectful that has the absence of pride and ego. The meekness of Christ will prevent us from using unnecessary force out of fear or anger. One of the biggest put offs for those into Wicca is a bombastic dogmatic forceful Christian.

Many an occultist has succumbed to pride as the devil gets his converts to feel powerful. After a blood sacrifice in Satanism a person can feel euphoria and intoxicated with a powerful adrenaline rush as the blood is shed. Often Occultist and spiritual devotees are made to feel they are extremely special with a gift or because they possess a spiritual gift, so only they can do a specific task that no one else can. This can lead to a sense of notoriety, loving to be in the lime light as many mediums and psychics do, loving to have their name up in lights and a large facebook following. They do generally believe they are good humble people helping others and saving the world. Little do these mediums and spiritual ones know it is all about a masquerade for something far more sinister.

For the deliverance minister or spiritual warrior they know without meekness they cannot defeat the demonic power. If you're going to inherit the earth or as the Greek reveals inherit the soil, the land, the region, the territory. Here and now there are towns, villages and cities the Lord wants to take back for Himself and he needs his saints to go and take the land back in His power and not in human strength and wisdom. God always seeks to work through his people for their good and his glory. If your home or street has been taken by the enemy humble yourself and take it back! A meek person will have a teachable spirit this will enable them to hear from the Lord and apply the word of God. By being meek you will gain spiritual intelligence from the throne room of heaven. Heaven is our Spiritual Headquarters. Once we have heaven's spiritual intelligence to what is going on and a strategic divine plan, we can step out in faith and take our promised land back for God's glory. Daily we must learn from God's Word. Our prayer life must be a two way communication of talking and hearing what the Lord is saying. Look at your own heart and ask just how teachable are you? Would you allow someone else to teach you? If you are an older Christian would you be meek enough to learn from a baby Christian something you have never seen before? Are we all willing to be meek and teachable from the Lord and His servants.

A meek person takes everything to the Lord in prayer they do not seek revenge and are not easily offended but they pray and let Jesus deal with the situation. Meekness teaches us to look at the situation from God's point of view so we may act accordingly. Many a person used by Satan will seek to undermine you, seek to ruin your reputation even use physical violence against you, cast spells and curses on you. Some will come into your home and church and leave something for a demon to attach itself to so the demon is not easily removed. Such objects can be revealed by the Holy Spirit and destroyed. Some under the demonic inspiration will smash up churches, even attack you. Again you do not take revenge and go out with a couple of heavy deacons with base ball bats. The Christian takes it all to the Lord in prayer. The pastor or elder has a duty of care to his congregation and makes sure things are as safe as possible. When necessary the police need to be informed when property is damaged, people threatened or attacked. But all the time we know we are fighting an invisible enemy who uses people like puppets on a string. Only the meek in Christ have strength and power to cut those strings. As the Meek are the ones who inherit the land.

The meek spiritual warrior is all ready to serve the Lord. Their life is lived for Jesus. Jesus comes first all the time and they are ready to serve him. When the Holy Spirit wakes you up at 2am to pray - you pray. When he prompts you to ask the lady serving at the till are you into spiritual things and she reveals she's into Wicca. The Lord is leading you to build a bridge to reach a wiccan for His glory. But all the time it's reaching out in meekness having great strength under control of the King of Kings. Your emotions and passions are under God's control as He uses you even when you're misunderstood. A warlock may mock, blaspheme and curse the beautiful name of our Lord and a flash of anger rises up in us at what they have said. But the meek have their anger under the control of the King of Kings so they can respond in the right way as they have allowed Christ to master them. Meekness helps to keep the Christian's testimony from being tarnished by their own foolishness.

Often in deliverance ministry the Lord will put you into a situation where only total dependence on Christ can bring about freedom. This humbles us as we can do nothing in our own strength.

She stood there at the edge of the village. Hearing the singing of gospel songs she came over and heard the gospel preached. She came forward for prayer. Instantly she fell to the floor and thrashed around like a wild animal. As gently as we could we held her to prevent her from harming herself, this lasted for about an hour. The sun would set over the banana trees before long, we had to wrap things up but she was not free.

She calmed down from being so crazy, we let her stand up. She ran and fell onto the dust floor about fifty meters from us. I saw her start thrashing again. With two other brothers we ran over and picked her up and brought her back under the trees and onto a mat. She was covered in dust that stuck to her through perspiration. We managed to bind the demons so she would not be harmed. It was a heart - breaking moment. Here we are preaching the power of the Gospel under an African sky and we could not set her free. Many previously had tried but to no avail. We left our small gospel meeting and went back to our hotel before dark. We made this situation a matter of prayer and fasting and arranged to meet this young girl at the end of the week, as we had no power.

Saturday arrived it was our D-day. The village had turned out to see what would happen. I can remember seeing high up in the tree a big bee's nest and praying that the demons would not throw it down on us. Before prayer we found out more about the girl, as Jesus would also ask some questions before a deliverance. The girl was being raised by her step mum. The parents had been into witchcraft, they had divorced so that her mother could become a witch doctor. Their daughter had been used in satanic rituals. Sadly she had had her arms cut and goat's blood poured over her as well as many other terrible things as she was to become a bride of Satan. Somehow she had been rescued by the lady who was now her step mum and had joined her tribe. We led this girl in prayers and renunciation of the Devil. The village gathered around singing to the Lord and praying. She leapt into the air and was going to run, about eight men were needed to hold this thin small person as gently and firmly as possible. She was shaking us all, we had no power. Eventually she was lying on floor stiff as a board being gently held, the Lord gave the command with Holy Spirit power, "In the power of the resurrection of Jesus Christ stand up and come out and be gone," She rose up like a person treading on the end of a rake head she did not bend but came up like the handle of a rake. As the pastors pressed in with prayer this twisted spirit left with a scream. The young girl was set free by Jesus and now is doing well in school and living a normal

Christian life. In the process we were deeply humbled and cast upon the Lord Jesus, rejoicing greatly in the victory of the cross of Calvary as we were allowed to see His victory and a young girl have freedom in Christ. Blessed are they in battle.

Chapter 4

Matthew 5:6

"Blessed are those who hunger and thirst for righteousness, for they shall filled".

She was tall and attractive with an ethereal kind of beauty sitting in her New Age spiritual bookshop. Her gentleness was apparent and you expected to see fairy folk sitting on her antique cash register which added to the nostalgia of the fausty mysterious shop. Crystals and quirky statues with incense burning in front of them added an eastern quality. She was brought up from the shawl with esoteric books, the words of myth and legend, spell and curse dripped off the pages and into her open mouthed soul. She was hungry and thirsty for eternity and a connection with the divine. She was addicted to her passion of spirituality but frustrated that she could not fill the empty gaping void of her bottomless soul.

The lady above that I encountered seeks to find something eternal to satisfy her eternal soul, she searches day and night from her childhood for a satisfactory answer. King Solomon in

Ecclesiastes 3:11 wrote:

"He has made everything beautiful in its time. Also He has put eternity in their hearts, except that no one can find out the work that God does from beginning to end".

God has put eternity in our hearts/soul which creates a hungering and thirsting for him. Sadly many search for God in the wrong places. Amongst the New Age spiritual people I have found many are willing to go to places to get some spiritual enlightenment, packing the van up and heading to Stonehenge or the pyramids of Egypt or South America with the kids to feel a vibration and receive instruction from a spirit to help them ascend the Gnostic ladder. Others may spend a large amount of money to spend time under a guru or a guided meditation week. What these people are doing is putting themselves in a place for enlightenment, an experience or divine instruction. Sadly behind so much spirituality that appears peaceful and transcendent there is a deadly dark side that ensnares the mind and soul.
However it's the same soul searching principle for the man or woman who hungers and thirsts after God. If you honestly seek God then you

will find him because he has put that desire into your heart to search for him. We must put ourselves in the place of prayer, reading God's word and of fellowshipping with other Christians if we are to find God through Jesus Christ. We must desire God and to know Him. If you want to be struck by lightning put yourself where the lighting will strike you, on top the mountain with a selfie stick in your hand. Many a person has said, "If only Jesus would reveal himself to me then I would believe" but they are not putting themselves in the right place by truly hungering and thirsting for God. They have a laissez-faire whatever will be will be attitude. They know something is there but they do not purse. The New Ager looks in the wrong direction. There is nothing nicer than tasting good food. This is where we can give the New Age shop owner some Christian literature to read to taste and see that the Lord is good, to point their spiritual appetite in the right direction.

Hungering and thirsting for righteousness - What is it? Ultimately it's longing for Jesus, the righteousness of God and being made like Jesus. It's not the false rightness that we see around us displayed by some goodie two shoes who pretends to be perfect and ever so pious.

The Christian is clothed in the righteousness of Jesus Christ and walks in His steps of righteousness and that is pleasing to Almighty God and gives us God's favor. Hence when God the Father looks at the person who is Born Again of God's spirit He sees that they are clothed in the righteousness of Jesus Christ. The apostle Paul in Ephesians 6:14 speaks of righteousness as a breastplate. The breastplate covers the heart. The believer's heart is covered and protected by a breastplate of righteousness. The spiritual warrior knows what it is to be in right standing with God and allowed into God's holy presence and live. Hence the believer desires the Lord Jesus Christ more than anything in the whole galaxy.

If we did not have Christ's righteousness we would die in the presence of a Holy God. The righteousness of Jesus enables us to go into the Holy of Holies and dwell with God our Father. Satan cannot mess with our heart because we are clothed in Jesus and have a defence and offence in Christ. Our defence is that we are clothed with Jesus our righteousness in the battle around us. Secondly we walk in the righteousness of Jesus in the battle ground to accomplish His will here on earth. That which is right in God's sight is divinely approved. In the spirit when the enemy of Christ looks at us He sees the deep work of Jesus in our lives which we hunger and thirst for with all of our strength and might. As we long for Jesus He fills us and we become fully alive in Him. Therefore the beauty of holiness dwells within us.

Deliverance ministers seek to be right in every area of their lives and filled with Jesus. If there is an area of your life that is not right in God's sight then Satan will aggravate that area of your life to make you miserable and a pretender of the Christian faith. How often have we gone into prayer and fasting to intercede for someone to be delivered from demonic powers and the first thing the Holy Spirit does is to reveal your sin. The Holy Spirit does this so you may be put right with God and fully clothed in Jesus and then the power of God will flow through you. When you enter into the home that needs to be exorcised or a person needs deliverance, you stand there being fully approved by God because the righteous work of Jesus on the Cross for you is now covering you. Satan fundamentally hates this as you have no chink in your armour for him to oppress you and side track you from the task at hand. You therefore stand fully in the

power and protection of the Lord Jesus Christ. Rejoicing in the fullness we have in Jesus.
It's only Jesus that can satisfy our eternal soul with all that is of Himself. When Jesus fills us and we know him in the battle we are truly blessed. Often this righteousness clashes with the kingdom of darkness. Plus this righteousness of grace clashes with those into the cults who rely on good works. If we have at the Holy Spirit's leading, confirmed by the word of God gone to share the good news of Jesus in a temple, new age shop or gathering we can feel spiritually polluted and corrupted as we leave. This contamination is highlighted because we know the authentic and pure righteousness of the Lord Jesus Christ. The false righteousness that flows from self righteous people or a satanic righteousness is repulsive to the Christian because he knows Jesus. He hungers and thirsts and is filled so then the counterfeit is easily exposed because the believer knows what is approved of by the Holy Spirit as He works in our spirit and confirmed by the Word of God. When the spiritual pollution comes we put ourselves in the place to meet with God, we ask for cleansing power of the Blood of Jesus to wash over us and we worship the blessed Godhead

and read His Word. We hide in the abode of God and dwell there lifting up our prayers of intercession and praise because we needed to be filled afresh and made pure and holy in greater sanctification.

I remember meeting up with a dedicated practicing shaman in the United Kingdom. We had agreed to meet to discuss spiritual things. From the floor to the ceiling books on occultism lined the living room wall. A large area of the room was dedicated to her many gods of gold, silver, bronze and wood. A healing table set up for the next client to lie upon with posters and charts for acupuncture. As we were greeted the pupils of her eyes changed into diamond shapes like that of a lizard or cat. Her eyes quickly reverted back to normal once the spirit had seen from within her who was calling. Her manner and smile became seductive with a strange impure sexiness. We shared the Gospel but her ears were sadly closed to the truth as she would interrupt saying the spirits don't like you, the spirits are swearing at you. She chose to listen to her spirits and began talking about what they wanted to tell us about ascended masters and that's all that Jesus was a, spiritually evolved person. As we stood to leave after a two hour discussion we were leaving feeling a little frustrated at not getting anywhere and feeling spiritually polluted. As we so wanted her to accept the Lord Jesus. I glanced at her book shelf and there in the middle of all the occultist books was an old children's Bible with a tattered cover.

I asked her why she has a Children's Bible in her library. She said she had it given to her when she was a child in Sunday school and could not throw it out. In that room of darkness and spiritual pollution we were strongly protected by the righteousness of Jesus, where His word sits on a shelf calling to her to know the true way. Praise God for the faithful Sunday School teachers around the world, their ministry remains with every child for a life time. When we left we rested and refreshed ourselves in the Lord Jesus. We desperately wanted to be in Jesus' holy presence away from the impure, twisted, vile demonic works of Satan. She saw her spirits as helpers and friends and would not leave them. Driving home and returning back home we hungered and thirsted for righteousness. Throughout the rest of the day we desired more of Jesus and for his salvation to come to lost shamanic spiritual healers who have eternity in their hearts but are looking in the wrong direction. We are to go into all the World and share the Gospel of Jesus Christ. Blessed are they in Battle.

Chapter 5

Matthew 5:7

"Blessed are the merciful, For they shall receive mercy".

We met in a secret location, Stan was dressed in black with deeply wicked dyed black hair. He struggled with mental health issues and followed Satanism boasting in the power of the left hand path. He had a vile hatred towards Christians and encouraged vandalism of Christian Churches. He hated Christian leaders with a venom. A few weeks ago by a miracle of grace He had asked Jesus into His life. Now I was meeting him as he held a plastic Tesco shopping bag full of letters written in blood to be sent to Pastors all over the world. We burnt the blood written correspondence and destroyed other satanic items for dark rituals. He struggled with Christian faith at first. My phone would ring and there would be threats and blasphemies spewing forth. A steady stream of love, grace and mercy was shown to Stan and now he is walking for Jesus freed from Satanic activity but still struggles with mental health issues. Great is the mercy of God which has been shown to him through the local Church.

In Matthew 5:7 the Christian is to have an attitude or a state of mind of mercy evident in their character because they too have received mercy from God. Mercy looks at the damage that sin does and has sympathy and compassion on that person. Mercy gets stirred in our hearts and wants to help take the burden that sin's damage has caused in a person's life. Mercy enables kindness to be shown, as in the parable of the Good Samaritan in Luke's Gospel 10:25-37. If we have received mercy from Christ then we should be merciful to those around us and continue in the battle to receive mercy in order to be merciful. Mercy has feet and hands. Mercy is something that is practical and puts things into action for a person's relief. To be merciful is the opposite of revenge.

The warrior of the Lord demonstrates mercy out of a work of the Holy Spirit in their own heart. They look at the world around them and see that humanity is dominated by the weight of sin and Satan. They are looking at the world as Christ Jesus would look at the world. A beautiful place that has been corrupted to its core . The church should reflect mercy. In a Church where religious spirits are controlling, mercy will be swapped for manipulation, legalism and control. The root of mercy flows out of the love of Jesus in a believer's heart, religious spirits seek their own self importance and power. The person in need of mercy and rescuing from the impact of sin can meet a person with a pharisaical spirit in a religious person. This religious spirit seeks to condemn and judge that person so they never feel peace and free by God's grace. A merciful person will see what the Lord is doing in that person's life and seek to rejoice with that person, in the fact they have both been forgiven for their sin and are set free now by the blood of Jesus. The past has gone and now they walk in the kingdom of heaven, the abode of God here on earth. Mercy is a characteristic of Jesus Christ and must be seen in our churches and lives. Do we see this attitude of mercy or is there always the dull dread of judgment and condemnation like a repetitive record so you never feel good enough and enjoy the mercy of our Lord. The church today needs to have the reality of the beatitudes to conquer religious controlling spirits. Without the beatitudes religious spirits will make people think they are God's chosen, when in fact they are in the flesh and carnal, resulting in pseudo believers who are killing the likeness of Jesus' mercy in action. The amazing thing is God is even willing to show mercy to religious legalistic controlling Pharisees. This is seen in the apostle Paul's life. Hence when we are not shown mercy we must not fall into the trap of not showing mercy back. The people who condemned us need mercy just as much as we do even if they hold a church office.

In battle every Born Again Christian has the capacity to show mercy and Christ is cultivating a merciful attitude in every Christian. For those who major in the area of deliverance that person may find they actually have a gift of mercy as seen in Romans 12:3-8. Romans 12:3-8 reveals 7 spiritual gifts that are to be found in the local church. Every Church member has at least one of these spiritual gifts. In the context of gifts from Father God verse 8 reads "he who shows mercy, with cheerfulness". A gift of mercy can be a foundational gift in deliverance ministry as one is motivated by mercy to relieve the suffering of the demonically subjected. If we have this gift of mercy then we are not going into deliverance for an exciting time to fight the devil, when we would generally lose. 1 Peter 1:10 says " Each of you should use whatever gift you have received to serve others, as faithful stewards of God's grace in various forms". Often when the deliverance minister with a gift of mercy has a phone call or someone calls to the church for help, the mercy gift kicks in and there is a deep sense of concern. The concern can be highlighted if children are being affected by the demonic. A mercy gift that gives you a concern for the demonically affected will also give you leading and purpose as it's a foundation built by God in your life.

A mercy foundation flows out of the love of Jesus in your life . Mercy highlights compassion and concern. The mercy gift enables you to respond in love and the afflicted feel they can trust you and open up about the evil that is going on with confidence and hope. Some things may be embarrassing for them to share but mercy flowing through you enables a person to share the satanic embarrassment to bring that which is hidden into the light is an act of mercy. Mercy does not treat us as we deserve. Mercy enables us to feel the person's pain so that we may help. Mercy is linked to being discerning to help understand what is going on in the person's situation. This helps trust to be built and an empathy as to what is going on.

The gift of mercy is a powerful gift and we need the Lord to help understand how the gift of mercy works. As we mature in mercy so our understanding will increase about this powerful gift. It now makes sense to me that when I read an article like in the National Geographic July 2017 about how people are going to spiritual healers for healing in Venezuela due to a desperate shortage of medication, or voodoo healers in the Republic of Benin or the local shaman doing a house cleansing, I naturally want to go and tell them of Jesus and see Jesus work in a powerful way and see His truth break in and set captives free. I now know this flows out of a gift of mercy wanting these people to be free from a terrible affliction of Satan. I desperately want people to have the real work of God and not the counterfeit from the wrong source. Praise God, He places us in the Body of Christ His Church to help give spiritual direction and spiritual balance. Mercy, Wisdom and discernment all need to work together as it's easy to find ourselves trying to put out too many fires at one time. The merciful can sometimes rush off into a situation rather than first seeking Christ. Hence we must pray for wisdom to know how to use the powerful spiritual gifts of the Father in the correct way.

At times we have to trust that God has his people in the right place at the right time to minister. No one person has the monopoly on deliverance. Satan would inflate our ego to think we are the only one who can set captives free. The truth is you are not the only person on the planet that can cast out demons and bring relief. James 5:16 is true "Therefore confess your sins to each other and pray for each other so you may be healed. The prayer of the righteous person is powerful and effective". As we pray we can all cast out the enemy in Christ's authority: Mark 16:17 "And these signs will follow those who believe: In My name they will cast out demons; they will speak with new tongues".

Mercy will help you to discern if the problem is being dealt with as your heart will have a unity with that person. This is due to the sensitive nature of the gift of mercy. As mercy is sensitive this can also mean we get hurt by harsh criticism of our ministry from people who often do not understand. When this happens the merciful tend to become quiet and seek their own company and to be with Jesus as their cheerfulness and their readiness to respond willingly has been grieved and dampened. The merciful thus receive mercy from Christ Himself to keep on showing mercy to those whom the Lord leads them to or draws to them.

He could not stay in the Sunday service, he would often go outside or hide in the toilets not really understanding why. But it always happened that way just before the preaching of God's precious Word. The elders noticed this, knowing this man wanted to follow Jesus, and yet Sunday after Sunday he would hide somewhere. One evening during church he was hiding in the toilet cubicle again. The elders waited for him to come out after the service and led him into the church office to pray for him. As soon as he stepped into the office he launched his attack, fists flying at the minister. Before a punch could land on the minister's nose, at the Name of Jesus this young man hit the floor like a sack of King Edwards potatoes being dropped from a great height. His fists still punching out. The elders instinctively jumping out of the way in surprise as church members quickly left the building. Merciful prayers were uttered to the throne of grace. There was no freedom or release found from the demonic subjection in that first meeting.

But in the second meeting repentance was able to be made, renouncing occult activity. Then the freedom from voodoo came. The young man said it was like a bolt of lightning hitting him which went right through his body. This man could physically feel chains being snapped off of him. This was the beginning of freedom for him all because the elders had mercy on him. They could have just let him hide and walk away and never deal with the root problem. Mercy brought freedom and victory. Mercy also brought a unity so the man could become an active part of the church and be free from spiritual torment. Blessed are they in battle who have the right attitude in God's kingdom and reflect the mercy of Lord Jesus Christ.

Chapter 6

Matthew 5:8

"Blessed are the pure in heart, For they shall see God".

He fell to the floor, as a sound of a snake came up from his core and out of his mouth, writhing on the floor, grabbing a chair leg and hurling a chair. All self control had been lost as the Babylonian spirit took full control of the man's body. At the name of Jesus the spirit was expelled, the prayer team in the next room interceded. After the exorcism the man was dazed with snippets of memory flashing back to what had just gone on. His legs were cut and scratched, he immediately went for a shower feeling free but a little embarrassed with a deep sincere sense of purity and holiness in his freed soul that he had never known before.
To have tasted the purity and holiness of Father God is a wonderful thing. The work of the cross leads to revealing our spiritual poverty leading us to satisfaction in God in our heart and mind. The heart is key in spiritual warfare, if your heart is not right with God then you will grieve

a work of the Holy Spirit. If your heart has unforgiveness, bitterness, jealousy, murder, or adultery then you leave yourself wide open for demons to harass you and agitate your wounds. By being in sin or habitual sin your mind has too many doorways for the enemy to attack you resulting in yourself becoming oppressed. The heart in scripture is emphasised time and time again that it must be made clean. The religious people just look at the exterior but Jesus always looks at the heart. Jesus often challenged the motives of the Pharisees of his day as they were concerned about the outward appearance and a show of religion that had no power. But the heart that is right with God and had been cleansed anew has power and intimacy with God. Using the brains God has given you is a good thing but the heart is what Jesus looks at. Whatever you do for the Lord has to flow from a pure heart.

You cannot make your heart clean and pure, you have to confess sin to the Lord and repent and be washed in the power of the blood of Jesus. Satan hates purity with a capital "H" for hate. Satan is the god of this world and seeks to pervert and suppress all that is good and confuse the mind about the true power and beautify of purity. When you encounter the

Purity of God you discover how impure your own heart is and mercifully receive a pure heart from Jesus. When you are dealing with a survivor of the occult you begin to see the work of purity deepen in their lives as they accept Jesus and walk in His footsteps. I often check by listing to see in the course of conversation if there is a revulsion to things that are satanic or a sense of pride in satanic ways and symbolism.

Often a Person under demonic subjection will aggressively shout out and blaspheme the name of Jesus because they hate the Presence of a Holy God and all that the name of Jesus stands for, as the name of Jesus reveals Jesus' character and work. Sometimes as you engage with different occultist its possible as you sit with them to feel an unclean spirit at work, your mind becomes polluted with sexual filth, there can be a strange energy that would push you towards that person. But the heart of the spiritual warrior that is pure finds a Holy resistance is stirred up in them to pull back and plead the blood of Jesus over themselves and asks for Jesus to stand between them and the person who may not even know that an unclean spirit is at work through them. I have encountered these twisted unclean spirits and found the point of entry into a person's life is through some sort of immoral activity or a connection with those who are engaged in gross sexual misconduct . By being pure in heart there is a natural revolution and you want to stay away hence this is a strong indicator than an unclean sprit could be present, and if possible would seek to ensnare you.

However knowing our poverty of Spirit and the fact that a Christian dwells in the abode of God, the kingdom of heaven, we have divine protection as we yield our will to Christ. It's so important if we are going to minister in the area of the demonic that we meditate on what is pure and holy so we can resist such an attack. It's an embarrassing situation not to have confessed your sins and have a person controlled by a demon start naming your sins. I know this happened once as a man was arrested by the police. Under clairvoyant inspired power he began to tell the officers who they were having an affair with in the police station. The police soon took him home and I met with the man the next day.

To be pure in heart means your personality is pure at its core. Hence your motives will be pure and wholesome. Again an unclean spirit will try and twist and pervert the personality to make a person rude and crude, suggestive and seductive. If you meet someone who is always crude, their sinful nature may be opening their mind up to becoming obsessed with uncleanness/filth and be gradually taken over by an unclean spirit. This is why we must be careful what we watch and say. Jesus said in Mark 7:21 "For from within, out of the heart of man, come evil thoughts, sexual immorality, theft, murder, adultery". What flows from our mouth, what we say and look at are a good indicator whether our heart is pure. If you are going to challenge the demonic it is paramount that your heart is pure. If your heart is not pure you will be open to being embarrassed or harmed physically or psychologically.

When dealing with sexual demons such as Incubi and Succubae it is paramount that your Christian walk with the Lord is one of purity. Ministry in this area involves trust and confidentiality as the person often feels great shame and embarrassment. In the history of religion it's documented that incubus attacks ladies sexually and succubus attacks men sexually. These spirits can enter a home through sexual sin, perversion or demonic contact involving satanic rituals even through the Ouija board! I have prayed with couples who have been involved in none of the above sins but were attacked by such sexual demons when they moved into a new property. Sometimes these spirits will attack children. When this happens every avenue sensitively must be explored to come to the right conclusion. This may not be a case of demonic sexual assault but human wicked child abuse as the child is being told that the perpetrator is a demon. I heard recently of one child abuser who would dress up in a devil outfit for Halloween. The child did not think it was their uncle but Satan himself coming into his bedroom at night. In dealing with such cases a person's culture must be also be taken into consideration to come to the correct diagnosis. If there is demon present then this can be expelled at the name of Jesus and any pornography burnt. If its human child abuse the correct authorities must be informed and the child protected.

Being pure in heart is a great defence against the demonic and makes demons shudder because they see the work of the cross in the deliverance minster's life and that power of the cross is now being applied in a pure motive to the one needing deliverance. The pure in heart

reflect the character of the Lord Jesus as they are clothed in righteousness and holiness. When vile oppression seeks to attack the deliverance pastor it is confronted with the Holiness of Jesus. When such spiritual attack arrives praise the Lord in the beauty of holiness as God inhabits the praises of his people. It should be of no surprise that when we conduct our meeting and the Holy Spirit is present and the Holy Word of God expounded that the unclean demonic cry out for they hate all that is holy and pure belonging to the King of Kings.
The believer is blessed with a glorious promise that they shall see God. Jesus said "If you have known me, you will also know the Father. From now on you know him and have seen him" (John 14:7) and "He that has seen me has seen the Father (John 14:9). Our blessed promise is one of certainty that the blessed Godhead shall work in His unique way and we shall see our God because he has made us pure. When we step into the glory of heaven all sin and its effects will be completely removed from us. This body of flesh shall be made glorious. The most important event of your life is yet to come and you will see God . Hence John the Apostle would say to us "All who have this hope in them purify themselves, just as He is

pure (1 john 3:3). Yes only God can give us a pure heart but we have a responsibility to try and stop the rubbish from landing in our heart and minds.

I have personally found it profitable to meditate on and pray through Psalm 51 about how to have a clean heart . Especially when I know the exorcism will be a battle. I have used Psalm 51 in many cases involving the demonic. As some people have read this psalm they have felt chocked, gone blind, deaf, thrown the word of God across the room. One man handed me my Bible back after reading Psalm 51 and I expected to see his finger prints burnt into the leather cover of the Bible as there was such a strong reaction to the Holy Word of God. This led to deep repentance, cleansing from sin and free access into the presence of God.

When the pure presence of God comes down in a meeting God is going to do a deeper work. One year we had a man come to us at church, he heard voices in his head and felt things slide over his body. For one year he read the word of God and we prayed together once a week. By the end of the year the voices had stopped and the sliding over his body and peculiar sensations had all stopped. This man wanted to get baptised and invite his family and friends to come to the baptism and hear the Gospel of Jesus Christ. It was an amazing baptism service and the pure presence of the Lord was there. As we cleaned up after everybody had gone home we noticed on the floor burnt pieces of plastic from a pair of shoes. The following Sunday the man who was baptised brought his dad's shoes to the church for us to all see.

The shoes had melted as his dad was standing on holy ground. This dad when younger had been involved in a lot of Ouija board secession. The clash between the Kingdom of darkness and the Kingdom of light caused this man's shoes to melt. We rejoiced at how we were standing on holy ground. Sadly this father refused to accept Jesus into his life. Even non Christians who were there who saw the shoes at a later date were telling him he needs to repent and get right with the Lord. As of yet he has not accepted the Lord. But we were all humbled at the holy presence of God and privileged to know that the Lord is the one who patiently makes our heart pure. We are blessed in the battle with divine purity to see God.

Chapter 7

Matthew 5:9

"Blessed are the peacemakers, For they shall be called the sons of God"

Like clockwork. There in the capital city sitting behind the church reception desk by 8:45am was a Celtic Buddhist ready for her daily task. Taking the names of the people entering into the a newly furnished church hall. This may have seemed like a small activity taking people's names and email addresses but she believed if everyone played their part locally to save the planet there would be a global transformation. When the group of participants were booked in. The bell was rung with a flick of the wrist. Sitting in the lotus position with the tongue touching the top of the mouth plus thumb and index finger connected. Breathing in a silent rhythm upon their orange, blue and green foam mats in the sunlit hall as shafts of light shone through the skylights. All seemed in perfect harmony and sublime unison. There was a connection to the earth and everything in the universe. If only everyone on this beautiful big blue and green squiggly earth could connect then surely peace would fill the earth once again. As they began to chant in rhythm a feeling of intoxication came over them as they swayed gently in unison as energy flowed from their group to heal their precious city and mother earth. Little did they know that they needed to meet with the Prince of Peace. They had never heard of the Prince of Peace because no one went to tell them about Him. Jesus was just one of many gods. Sadly those who had the truth about true peace and spiritual healing could not be bothered and did not even care about lost souls and their own planet's future!

It's the blood of Jesus Christ that gives us peace with God the Father. Colossians 1:20 "and through him to reconcile to himself all things, whether on earth or things in heaven, by making peace through his blood, shed on the cross". So many groups like the one mentioned above are trying to use a sequence of techniques to find peace with God and bring peace to the earth. Whereas all they need is the cleansing blood of the Lord Jesus Christ. If they would apply the blood of Jesus they would have peace and become natural peacemakers with each other. Only through Jesus death can the entire cosmos be brought back to a state of peace. Until that day when peace robbers are removed the spiritual warrior seeks to bring peace wherever they go.

The deliverance ministry is one of bringing peace into a person's life and acts as a peacemaker. Peacemakers seek to help make people whole. The soul that is vexed and tormented by the demonic affliction is conquered by the blood of Jesus. Repetitive thought patterns, being touched, being afraid if the root is demonic the blood of Jesus can bring peace and relief from such torment by the application of the blood of Jesus. The blood of Jesus removes all sin hence removing any anchor point for the demonic attachment resulting in freedom and peace. It goes without saying the deliverance ministers must know this personally for themselves and must not be an antagonistic quarrelsome pain in the neck type of person which is the opposite of a true Holy Spirit empowered peacemaker.

Being a Peacemaker in deliverance is something that is active. Many a believer can be attacked by a spirit of weariness and slumber and do not look for an opportunity to be a peacemaker or actively guard the peace that already is in existence. Before going into a spiritual battle the deliverance minister may be lazy and lethargic and not spend quality time in prayer and the word of God and checking his own heart before God. He also needs to see if the Holy Spirit wants to pre warn him about something or give some key insight for the subjected person to be set free. If we want to bring peace we must watch and pray. Sleeping on the job can lead to times of darkness and destruction. Our aim and joy should be to serve Christ to see men and women be reconciled to God and set free to follow the Prince of Peace.

Prayer is a way of bringing peace into someone's life. If I personally begin to feel sleepy in prayer then I get up and walk around praying indoors or outdoors. When you go to minister to a person and you enter into where they are what do you discern? Is there a passive atmosphere that makes you sleepy and comfortable? This can be a false spirit of peace at work which connects people to each other in mystical demonic bondage. This spirit has prevented you from using your mind to discern what is going on. Often this is experienced when dealing with spirits linked to meditation and mind control groups. The spirit of peace from the Lord Jesus is light and does not dull your sense and mind. The spirit of Jesus does not make you passive so you embrace and accept everything. A false demonic peace is often heavy and makes the mind passive. The deliverance minister's mind reacts to such an atmosphere. The discerning Christian know the peace of Jesus in a room, and can discern what is a demonic peace, and when tiredness is natural and not a lulling into sleep caused by a spirit.

Being a peacemaker means when you see the local witch or occultist you are courteous and kind and seek for them to be reconciled to God in a genuine authentic way. You're not there to persecute devil worshippers as some Christian groups do and have done! These are men and women made in the likeness of God and they have gone astray as sin works in them. If you are antagonistic and they feel persecuted by you, when they need help where will the go? If all we have done is behave in an unloving non Christian way. Many an occultist has a wrong view of the Born Again Christian because all they have encountered is a religious dogmatist. If you pass a person in the street, even giving a smile, can be an act of being a peacemaker as you make a very simple connection that may later lead to an opportunity to share the good news with them. In Africa you may even help to secure and make the home safe where albino children live so that they may feel safe from those who would seek to catch them and sell them. Albino children are a target as their body parts are needed for magic potions. The deliverance minister must be practical as well as spiritual in peacemaking. Peacemakers are friendly people who are approachable and do all they can to bring about peace. The peacemaker uses words, actions and prayer to produce peace to point others to Christ. Romans 14:19, "Therefore let us pursue the things which make for peace and the things by which one may edify another". In conflict peacemakers try to remain neutral and not take sides so that Jesus is seen and the reconciling power of Jesus' blood can flow. The peacemaker has done away with their own ego and self interest. They are not saying what can I get from this situation. The peacemaker is willing to lay down his own desire and ambition to see freedom and reconciliation come between two people. The peacemaker does not think to themselves, "Oh when this person is delivered from Satan's grip, people will hear about it and think what a powerful Christian I must be, and I'll get lots of phone calls to go and minister in different churches and countries". This is pride and a desire for popularity which will hinder the work of God through you. The peacemaker has crucified their pride and desire to be a big important person, because it is the nature and character of Satan and certainly not fitting for a deliverance minister who should be representing the Lord Jesus Christ in a Peacemaking capacity. The deliverance pastor must decrease and Christ increase. The deliverance minister's main concern is that Jesus is glorified and seen in all things because it's only the Holy Spirit who can bring true peace into the situation.

The Kingdom of darkness is one of violent innocent bloodshed. The kingdom of God is the complete opposite as in God's Kingdom His children dwell, the sons and daughters of the Living God. If we are God's peacemakers then we are given the privilege of being called the children of God, Romans 8:16 "The Spirit Himself testifies with our spirit that we are the children of God". We are also sons and daughters adopted into God's family and in his family there is peace. If we are called then we are owned by God in a positive sense. Being belonging/owned by God, walking as peacemakers in his kingdom, gives the deliverance minister a tremendous sense of security and peace that he/she belong to God.

As God is your Father and you're His son or daughter then he is watching you all the time and He sees what is going on physically, emotionally and Spiritually and is right there with you when confronting powers of darkness that seek to hold his image bearers captive. God desires for His children to reflect and conform to the image of His Son.

The new pastor came forward for prayer he began to shake violently, the deacons held him gently but firm as they could. His body began to writhe as the demonic began to reveal itself in its hideous way. He was grinding his teeth as his face became dog like in appearance, something I've seen now around the world in ministry. As we prayed things got worse and there was no peace, he had not slept properly for nights, and others began to fear him in his own church and wondered if they had appointed the right man to lead them. The man and church had no peace. Getting nowhere we calmed him down and asked if he needed to confess anything, he confessed his involvement in paying witch doctors to meet his needs. Upon repentance and confession the blood of Jesus was applied and this dog demon left. The Lord had brought deliverance and the peace of Jesus came upon this man's mind and body.

Also his church had peace now this man was free from the powers of the witch doctor and demons.

Chapter 8

Matthew 5:10

"Blessed are those who are persecuted for righteousness' sake for theirs is the kingdom of heaven".

I arrived in South India having been greeted at the airport with a garland of orange flowers being placed around my neck. The Christian brothers and sisters were warm and friendly. The mission trip to India was going well with baptisms in the sea and many precious souls turning to Christ as their Savior. Special permission was granted to have Gospel crusades and meetings in the local villages. I slept in a local orphanage where many children had been rescued from the jungle. As we travelled by motor bike I wanted to stop in one local village to do evangelism but the local pastor was too well known and would be attacked by the local fundamental Hindu people. Previously Christians had boldly proclaimed the gospel in the village and were violently attacked with sticks. The local pastor was afraid we would be pulled off the motor bike and beaten with sticks for just being Christians going through the village. The local village Hindus believed attacking Christians was a way of showing devotion and allegiances to the local Hindu deities. The year before an Australian missionary family had been burnt alive as they slept in their car heading to the mission station by radical Hindus.

When you begin to follow Jesus and your character becomes like His, you naturally do the things that Jesus did. Christians become the hands and feet, ears and mouth of Jesus here on earth. Hence you can be persecuted for being like Jesus, such a tremendous complement. When people start getting set free from the demonic through the ministry the Lord has given you, some Christians will not understand and say that it was all mental illness that we don't encounter demons today, and that there is no such thing as a demon, that it's superstition. Others will say there is no such thing as a personal devil. Satan will try and bring confusion into the church and legalism to prevent a work of the Holy Spirit preventing the Kingdom of heaven coming in power, thus keeping lost souls in spiritual darkness.

Persecution here in Matthew 5:10 can refer to a hunter quickly pursuing its catch. Satan wants to destroy all followers of Jesus Christ simply because they reflect the Lord Jesus' righteousness. There is a clash of kingdoms between light and darkness. Satan uses fear and Jesus conquers in love and has clothed his sons and daughters in righteousness and Satan personally hates that. You can be a crystal gazing, tree hugging, save the planet, goddess worshipper, full of good deeds and eastern calmness and no one will bat an eyelid. Say you're born again and people think you're weird and ridicule you. Being born again and clothed in the righteousness of Jesus is going to upset any unclean spirit, because when you walk in the room that unclean spirit sees the pure heart that Christ has made in you and that unclean demon is enraged at the sacred and divine work of the cross of Calvary.

The demons are reminded of where they once stood and how they have fallen and are defeated by Jesus' death and resurrection. Hence they are repulsed by the genuine work of the Holy Spirit in a believer and they fear and tremble at it. Therefore they seek to mock and ridicule the church and persecute the righteous sons and daughters of the living God. Don't think it a strange thing if you get persecuted for saving souls and seeing captives set free, it goes with the territory. And when persecution comes the Holy Spirit will strengthen you to do and say the right thing in that moment. The martyrs that have died for their faith were all supernaturally empowered by the Holy Spirit. Every country in the world has the martyrs blood upon it even in the United Kingdom.

We are in a spiritual battle with a capital "B". Satan will throw all he can at us. But Satan is limited in power and what he can do. He can only go as far as God allows him to go. Satan is like a big dog on a lead, he can only go so far, he is restricted to what he can do by our heavenly father who is in full control.

Persecution arises out of the issue of loyalty and to whom you will be faithful. For example the early Christians would not embrace the worship of Serapis sometimes pronounced Sarapis. Sometimes we see Serapis' statue in restaurants. Serapis was a popular Egyptian Greek god. Serapis wore a robe and had a big curly beard, he had a scepter in one hand and rested his other hand on a three headed dog called Cerberus. Cerberus was known as a very big watchdog who would eat anyone who tried to escape Hades. Serapis and Cerberus were well known in Greek mythology, the religion of the day throughout Greek culture. If you were invited for a meal it was common practice for the first glass of wine to be offered and poured out to the god Serapis. At this point the Christians loyalty would be tested. Devotion to Jesus or compromise and embrace the Egyptian Greek god Serapis and his big dog. Choosing to be loyal to Jesus would mean being excluded from the meal and fellowship with friends. More than likely your friends would turn against you and shun you for not offering wine to a false mythological god.

Separating yourself from the worship of false gods leads to persecution and isolation whether they are African, Greek, Roman, or Eastern gods. To be loyal to Christ can be extremely difficult at times. Even in the UK. I've known it to be hard for teenagers who have come to faith when their parents are practicing Spiritualist or devoted Buddhist. When you're a child or a teenager being taken to the temple or spiritualist church you don't have much say in the matter but your heart can still be focused on the Lord Jesus and a praying church for you is paramount. Often in Africa we will tell Muslim children about the Lord and share bible stories, so they have an understanding for when they are older and can ask Christ into their lives. I've know some children to ask Jesus into their lives, they go home and say to their Muslim parents they have become Christians and they have received harsh beatings. Hence we try to convert the head of the family first.

I personally believe that a lot of persecution is demonically inspired. As 1 John 5:19 says "And we know that we are of God, and the whole world lies in wickedness [or, in the wicked one]". The Christians lives in the Kingdom of heaven now and in the future. If we are truly living in the Kingdom of God we will be exposing the works of the wicked one reviling what is sin and the demonic. Hence a clash of Kingdoms and a clash of loyalties. The believers keep their focus on Christ and heaven as their reward.

A Satanic inspired persecution inflames the anger and hatred of men and women's hearts to cruelly attack in varying degrees the Christian whose righteousness is that of Jesus Christ's. Deep in the heart of the true believer is a knowledge that the Kingdom of heaven belongs to them. The believer does not seek to be persecuted or draws attention to themselves but considers it a privilege to suffer for Jesus because great will be their reward in heaven.

The heavy darkness pressed in upon the pastor

and his wife as they had taken into their home a new Christian saved out of paganism. They were an extreme pagan group that held to blood sacrifice and mingled Satanism with druidic beliefs. The phone rang on its rickety stand. It was a warning they are going to kill Blue for leaving them. Later that night cars could be heard revving their engines outside the house to intimidate those inside, when going to the shops they were shouted at and intimidated by having hand guns waved at them. Arriving home the house had been broken into and paint thrown everywhere. Again the phone would ring, when answered they would hang up. Letters of threats were sent to their home and their vehicles damaged. Visiting Christians were also starting to be targeted by this extreme group driven by demonic subjection. The pastor's Church also became a target as vandalism was carried out and symbols of the all seeing eye drawn boldly onto different parts of the building. The congregation began to experience disunity as petty quarrels were starting to break out in the church as some could not discern the spirit of dissention being projected against the church members. Some of the pagan group would threaten church members for their part in converting Blue to Christianity. Blue changed his name and moved away to live out his Christian faith away from the threat and persecution. It was an extremely stressful time in the ministry for the pastor and his wife and Blue. For those who were walking with the Lord though this time of Occultist persecution they could testify to the Lord's goodness as they remained faithful to the Lord.

Contact

If you have any questions or need help about deliverance or a speaking engagements see the below and we will do our best to get back you.

Email riverwildrev@gmail.com

Phone Church Office 01443 693759

Write Jerusalem Baptist Church, Pentrebach, Castle Street, South Wales, CF48 4BN, UK

Printed in Poland
by Amazon Fulfillment
Poland Sp. z o.o., Wrocław